Trav
Reluctant Ghost Hunter
- stories from across Britain.

by
Joanna Jackson Cowell

THE GHOST & LEGEND SERIES

THE JOHN MERRILL FOUNDATION

THE JOHN MERRILL FOUNDATION,
32, Holmesdale, Waltham Cross,
Hertfordshire. EN8 8QY

Tel. 01992 - 762776
Email - marathonhiker@aol.com
www.johnmerrillwalkguides.co.uk
www.thejohnmerrillministry.co.uk

Registered Copyright logo.

TYPESET AND DESIGNED BY REVD. JOHN N. MERRILL.
PRINTED AND HANDMADE BY REVD. JOHN N. MERRILL.
BOOK LAYOUT AND COVER DESIGN BY REVD. JOHN N. MERRILL.

© COPYRIGHT - TEXT & PHOTOGRAPHS - JOANNA JACKSON COWELL. 2020

ISBN 978-1-8381125-0-9

FIRST PUBLISHED - JUNE 2020.

TYPSET IN FUTURA - BOLD, ITALIC AND PLAIN - 10PT, 14PT AND 18PT.

THE JOHN MERRILL FOUNDATION MAINTAINS THE JOHN MERRILL LIBRARY AND ARCHIVES AND ADMINISTERS THE WORLDWIDE PUBLISHING RIGHTS OF JOHN MERRILL'S WORKS IN ALL MEDIA FORMATS.

THE JOHN MERRILL FOUNDATION PLANTS SUFFICIENT TREES THROUGH THE WOODLAND TRUST TO REPLENISH THE TREES USED IN ITS PUBLICATIONS. PRINTED ON RECYCLED PAPER.

COVER PHOTOGRAPHS - ARDVRECK CASTLE, LOCH ASSYNT.

DEDICATION -

This book is dedicated to my mum and dad; my mum Jean for her interest in the paranormal and my dad Ken for his love of history.

Thank you for igniting my passion in them both.

Much love now and always.

CONTENTS

Page No.

Dedication 3
About the author 6
Introduction 7
CHESHIRE -
St. Boniface's Church, Bunbury, Nr. Chester 9
CORNWALL -
Jamaica Inn, Bolventor 11
DERBYSHIRE -
Alfreton's Old Gate Inn 13
Derby Goal 14
The Jessop's Monument and the Medieval Ghost! Codnor Park, Ironville 15
The Chapel of St. Mary on the bridge, Derby 17
GLOUCESTERSHIRE -
Tudor House Hotel, Tewkesbury 19
The Garrick's Head, Bath 20
LANCASHIRE -
Samlesbury Hall 21
LEICESTERSHIRE -
The Guildhall, Leicester 23
The Haunted Ruins of Grace Dieu Priory, Charnwood 25
Rothley Train Station, Rothley 26
STAFFORDSHIRE -
Tamworth Castle & The Lady's Chamber 30
LINCOLNSHIRE -
Epworth Old Rectory - Birthplace of Methodism & Old Jeffrey, the Poltergeist .34
Harlaxton Manor, near Grantham 36
RAF Coleby Grange, Matheringham 38
Temple Bruer, North Kesteven 39
LONDON -
The Nell Gwyn, Bull Inn Court, off The Strand 41
The Ten Bells, near Spitalfields Market - Jack the Ripper's local pub 42
NORFOLK -
Castle Rising 44
NORTHAMPTONSHIRE -
St, Mary's church, Woodford 45
The Talbot Hotel, Oundle 46
NORTHUMBERLAND -
Featherstone Castle's Haunted Tower and Chapel near Alston 47
NORTH WALES -
Llanbadrig, Anglesey 49

4

NOTTINGHAMSHIRE -

Annesley Hall and Old Church 50
The Bell Inn, Nottingham 52
Bestwood Lodge 53
Clifton Hall 55
Colwick Hall, Nottingham 56
St. Giles's Church, Holme - a visit to Nan Scott's Chamber" 57
Nags Head, Mansfield Road, Nottingham 59
Newstead Abbey 60
The Crying Angel, East Stoke 62
The Priory Church in Worksop 63
Rufford Abbey and the Black Friar 64
The Bessie Sheppard Memorial Stone, Mansfield Road, Nottingham 66
The Sunken Church, Bramcote 67
The White Hart Pub in Lenton, Nottingham 68

OXFORD -

The Haunted "Holt Hotel", Steeple Aston 69
Minster Lovell Hall, Witney 71
The Haunted Priory, Burford 73

RUTLAND -

Holy Trinity Church, Teigh 74

SUFFOLK -

The Haunted Friary, East Bergholt 75
The "Green Children" of Woolpit 76
Rendlesham Forest UFO Trail 77

YORKSHIRE -

Holy Trinity Church, Micklegate, York 78
Clapdale Hall, Clapham, North Yorkshire 80

SCOTLAND -

Ardchattan Priory, Argyll 81
Ardvreck Castle, Loch Assynt 82
Ballachulish House, Glencoe 83
Barcaldine Castle 84
Corgaff Castle, Aberdeenshire 85
The Drover's Inn, Inverarnan, Loch Lomond 87

ORBS 88
Footnote 89
With thanks 90
Bibliography 91
The Ghost and Legend Series 92
The Nottinghamshire Heritage Series 93
The John Merrill Foundation Book List 94

About the Author.

I've been interested in ghosts and other mysteries of the universe for as long as I can remember, and this was fuelled by my mum's books on the subject and my own vivid imagination. My own personal experience of the paranormal which I have detailed at the beginning of this book really sent my enthusiasm into over-drive, (despite it scaring me to death!) and made me determined to discover more.

I live in rural South Nottinghamshire with my husband Pete, who bravely (and patiently), assists me in my ghost hunting endeavours. I love travelling around our beautiful country taking photographs and finding out as much as I can about local history and folklore. I am also a Reiki, Crystal and Angel healer, both for people and animals.

I would welcome anyone who would like to be included in my next book to please get in touch, and if you'd like to keep updated with my various ghostly adventures around Britain (and hopefully very soon beyond), visit my Facebook page "the reluctant ghost hunter" and simply Like my page to get updates.

The Reluctant Ghost Hunter has a lot more travelling to come. Cheers!

Introduction

I would like to begin this book by saying a little about what inspired much of my journey into the mysterious world of ghosts and the unexplained. It was probably about 20 years or more ago now that my husband Pete and I took my mum away for the night to visit a relative and stopped overnight at The Old Ferry Boat in Holywell at St Ives in Cambridgeshire.

I wasn't too perturbed initially by the gravestone in the bar; it wasn't particularly obvious and was laid flat like a flagstone. Its strange presence was in regard to a very tragic tale regarding the death of a 17 year old girl called Juliet Tewsley. Due to unrequited love she was said to have committed suicide, and because of the manner of her death she was not allowed to be buried in hallowed ground. Although this was of interest I was not unduly worried, as I had heard no talk of ghosts.

We all then went on to have a pleasant evening meal in what was a warm, welcoming atmosphere, and then went up to bed. Fortunately my mum was in a bedroom that was not above the bar area, although she did say she felt dizzy and a bit light-headed on her way upstairs. (I want to re-iterate that none of us had drunk much alcohol that night, especially my mum who barely drank at all.)I had imbibed a couple of small glasses of wine and felt absolutely fine, just a bit tired and ready for bed. I had not been asleep very long when I awoke feeling as if the atmosphere in the room had completely changed. It was incredibly warm and stuffy, almost as though you could have cut it with a knife. I remember feeling unnerved, because this didn't seem right somehow, so I did a quick Reiki power symbol above my head to reassure myself before falling back to sleep.

The next morning everything appeared fine initially although the windows in the room had steamed up, of which I wasn't surprised considering the stuffiness during the night. But after going into the bathroom and then returning to bed I was suddenly hit by a tremendous wave of nausea. I ran back into the bathroom thinking I was going to be sick but thankfully I wasn't, but I couldn't understand why I felt so ill.

Pete suggested a walk outside along the river bank, which I hastily agreed to, and it was beautiful; birds singing, the sun shining, and I rapidly felt better as we returned to the inn. But then as I sat on the bed to watch TV while Pete went into the bathroom the nausea returned and I had to stand up. This was NOT normal, there was something awful about being in this room and my whole intuition was telling me I had to get out. This time I knew I did not want to return to the room once I had left, so while Pete and my mum had breakfast I sat outside the inn and inexplicably burst into tears. The sickness had gone now that I had left the room, although I was still in no mood for breakfast, but now the overwhelming feeling was one of sadness and grief. I had no idea what I was crying about, but I sat and sobbed for about half an hour until it was time to leave the hotel.

Finally, before leaving, I knew I wanted to do something to try and make things "right". I returned to the gravestone in the bar and did another Reiki power symbol over the slab. I have no idea if it made any difference but I like to think I at least tried to do something to calm the atmosphere. Although my experience terrified me, it also sparked my passion and interest for things we cannot explain. I would love to return to The Old Ferry Boat one day – perhaps I will, or perhaps I won't. That's why I call myself the "reluctant" ghost hunter.

St Boniface's Church, Bunbury, near Chester.

A 14th century Phantom Knight and a statue hidden by the vicar!

The village church at Bunbury near Chester contains the tomb and also reputedly the spectacular ghost of Sir Hugh de Calveley, a fearsome warrior knight from the 14th century. He stood 7 feet tall and could hold an anvil over his head. It is said that the tomb is damaged as the alabaster has been chipped away to be ground up and given as sheep medicine!

His ghost appears on a horse riding along the lane from his old manor at Calveley, continues up to the church where he dismounts and walks into the nave where he vanishes.

There is also the tomb of Jane Johnson who died in 1741 and celebrates her womanly figure! In 1760 the vicar thought it so improper (and distracting to the men-folk during his sermons) that he had the statue buried in the churchyard. In 1882 a gravedigger came across it and it was placed back in the church.

Jamaica Inn, Bolventor, Cornwall

Immortalised by Daphne du Maurier in her novel of the same name, Jamaica Inn stands isolated on the old coach road between Launceston and Bodmin.

The inn was built in 1547 as a farm, then in 1750 became a coaching inn. It then became a Temperance House before more recently reverting back to an inn. Its unusual name came from the local landowning Trelawny family, two of whose members served as Governors of Jamaica in the 1700s.

Smugglers stopped here on their journeys across the moor or to hide their goods, its isolation making it ideal.

Ghostly hoof-beats of a coach and horses have been heard on the cobbled courtyard, along with the sounds of heavy objects being unloaded.

On foggy nights the figure of a man on horseback has been seen waiting outside, and also seen is the ghost of a man who was set upon and murdered here by a gang of thieves. His ghost was first reported in 1911.

There is also a green cloaked man, a young mother and baby who haunt room 5, mysterious footsteps late at night and a man in a tricorn hat!

Alfreton's Old Gate Inn, Derbyshire

This welcoming stone building on the High Street in Alfreton dates from the 1600s and was originally the Gate Inn, before becoming a residential property and then coming under the ownership of the County Council.

In the 1970s it was partly leased to the Royal Voluntary Service, and from around that time talk began of ghostly goings-on including the sound of phantom footsteps. Today it is a cafe which I obviously had to try out for myself, just for investigative purposes obviously. You may notice this becomes a recurring theme, (only surpassed by my appreciation for a good pub).

Derby Gaol

Now a working museum, Derby Gaol was bought by paranormal investigator Richard Felix in 1997. It has been featured on Most Haunted and there have been many paranormal occurrences and sightings reported. Some guests just never want to leave...

The Jessops Monument and the Medieval Ghost! Codnor Park, Ironville, Derbyshire.

This is a momument dedicated to the memory of William Jessop, founder of The Butterley Company who developed the surrounding grounds.It was built in the 1850s and was a popular attraction for galas and Sunday school outings. Inside was a spiral staircase which led to a viewing platform at the top.In July 1861 the momument was hit by lightning and was so badly damaged that it was eventually closed to the public. But then comes the tale of the ghost...

I have been passed confidential information (oh yes I have!) from an investigators report which took place in 1997. Apparently a group of surveyors were escorted to the site due to plans for opencast mining, and the original plans were to demolish and rebuild the Monument after the work was completed. While surveying the area a man on horseback in medieval costume was seen near the monument who began throwing stones at the group and then vanished into thin air. From then on the surveyors equipment would not operate correctly.

I would have loved to have approached the Monument for a closer look but unfortunately it is fenced off with quite a few aggressive "Keep Out – Big Dogs About" type of signs. Although this happened quite a few years ago now I find the story and its subsequent report quite intriguing. If anyone has heard of anything to do with this case or any other paranormal activity here I would love to hear from you.

The Chapel of St Mary on the Bridge, Derby.

Near this place on 24th July, 1588, Nicholas Garlick, Robert Ludlam and Richard Sympson suffered martyrdom for their faith as Catholic priests.

Known as the Padley Martyrs (Padley Hall was where two of the priests were discovered), all three were hung, drawn and quartered, and Ludlam was the last of the three to be executed. He is said to have stood smiling, even while Garlick's execution was being carried out, and then said "Come, you blessed of God" just before he was thrown off the ladder. Their mutilated bodies were then displayed outside the chapel. The first chapel was probably built here in the late 13th century. The 15th century cell here was occupied by a hermit called John Shelton and his wife.

This little chapel is an undiscovered gem of a place, situated as it is on the outskirts of a busy city and after walking through a rather unprepossessing underpass to get there! You also need to check the opening times as the chapel is opened only on certain days by its fabulous volunteers and also for occasional services. But it is a place not to be missed, both for its heart warming, charming simplicity and also its bloody, thought-provoking history. Shown in the photo is my husband and ghost-hunting partner in crime Pete, admiring the brick work of the chapel, and doing his best to herd me on to one of the haunted pubs. (He really suffers for my hobby).

Tudor House Hotel, Tewkesbury

Dating back to the 16th century, The Tudor House Hotel appears to hold a number of ghosts. There is a staircase supposedly haunted by a barking dog, a woman who haunts the corridors at night and a breakfast room which used to be the courtroom for the town - with tales of guilty people being hung just outside the door in the courtyard!

Unfortunately (or fortunately) we were not stopping in the main hotel but in an annexe across the carpark which was disappointingly "non olde-worlde" if that is the correct expression! But the staff were extremely helpful and friendly, even with their own dossier on the hotel's ghosts! (Why can't every place be as organised with their history as this?) And I recommend their food too!

But I didn't detect any ghostly activity on the staircase or in the breakfast room, although the room was quite dark and not particularly cosy, so it was easier than it should have been to imagine it being used for issuing the death penalty!

The Garrick's Head, Bath - the Ghost of a Regency

Rake (and a sharp tongued usherette!)

This is the glamorous entrance to the former Garrick Head Hotel in Bath, which is now a pub. It was reputed to have been a gaming-house run by Beau Nash and linked by a secret passage to the neighbouring theatre. A regency rake is said to hover near the entrance, some think he is also responsible for the strong scented smell in the cellar, while others say it is from the ghost of a lady who committed suicide when her lover lost a duel in which she was the stake. There is also said to be a Grey Lady who threw herself out of a window. She is also seen in the Theatre Royal sitting in a box, but her identity is a mystery.

My attempts to enter the theatre to take a photograph of the said box were thwarted by an abrupt usherette who rather officiously refused me entry - how rude!!

Samlesbury Hall, Lancashire.

Grade I listed Hall built in 1325, with a history including Tudor priest holes, witches and various hauntings.

One of the ghosts is believed to be Dorothy, the daughter of Sir John Southworth, who was a staunch Catholic. Dorothy wanted to marry a squire from the neighbouring village who had abandoned his faith, and so her father was against the match. They planned to run away together but Dorothy's brother discovered what they were planning and murdered his sister's sweetheart.

Dorothy was banished to a convent abroad where she apparently went mad and died, but her restless spirit still roams the grounds and meets her lover to walk and embrace before they disappear. I hope this means they are reunited together at last.

Her ghost has even been spotted on the busy main road outside the grounds, with buses stopping to give her a lift!

Samlesbury Hall is an absolutely stunning place to visit with loads to see and a fabulous restaurant as well. (And no, they haven't paid me to say that).

The Guildhall, Leicester.

This beautiful ancient hall dates from around 1390 so there is plenty of history to support its reputation for ghosts.

A large, bearded man looking a bit dishevelled has been seen in the cells, wandering around in a confused state. (Although I'm afraid this sort of sighting might be quite common around most city centres, usually at chucking-out time). A ghostly dog haunts the courtyard, along with the sound of footsteps in heavy boots. And after extensive building work was carried out to create the cafeteria area, (which meant the removal of around 100 bodies from the private graveyard), chairs have been said to move on their own and the cafeteria bell rings of its own accord!

"Mary" is said to be the ghost that haunts the stairway leading to the library. Apparently she died after falling down these very stairs, and now she appears to be interested in the King James I Bible here and will turn the pages to her favourite passage.

The ghost of a black cat has also been seen here and is known to move about so quickly that it may "trip up" unwitting passers-by.

I love the Guildhall, both for its history and its grandeur, and it was here where I made my first foray into the world of professional ghost hunting. With the invaluable help of Marion and Dee from the local Leicester Progressive Spiritualist Church I set up a "Spirited Soiree" here one evening a few years ago. It didn't go quite as I'd planned it, and cost me far more money than I would ever have made back, but it made my dream a reality and we had a lot of fun (and cake!) Would I do it again? Never say never, but next time I want Prosecco, and preferably some ghosts...

The Haunted Ruins of Grace Dieu Priory, Charnwood, Leicestershire.

Grace Dieu Priory was founded in the 13th century by Roesia de Verdon as a house for nuns. It lasted nearly 300 years until the dissolution of the monasteries in 1538.

It is known for being one of the most haunted locations in Leicestershire, with numerous accounts pertaining to a lady in white (the colour worn by the nuns). Many drivers have seen and even stopped to offer a lift to the woman, after which she then disappears.

Rothley Train Station, Rothley, Leicestershire.

I have been reading about the ghost stories of Rothley train station in Leicestershire from the excellent book "Railway Ghosts and Phantoms" by W.B.Herbert.

I was lucky enough to meet a lovely gentleman called Roy who was a good friend and workmate of Stuart Bailey, an ex station master of Rothley, mentioned in the book as having heard many tales of the supernatural.

There appears to be several ghosts present at the station, including one startling experience which happened just a few weeks ago, and of which I will divulge with the following photographs...

There are several ghost stories related to this train station, one being the tale of a man walking home in the early hours of the morning and seeing the ghost of a station master or porter waiting for a train at 2am on a Sunday morning, of which obviously no service was running.

Another ghost story is that of a man and his dog at Swithland which is close to Rothley. Before World War II a local man used to cross over the railway lines with his dog to avoid the muddy morass beneath the bridge. But one night in the early years of the war both he and his dog were killed by a passing train. From then on the ghosts of both this man and his canine companion have been seen on many occasions, and the story is still talked about to this day.

Roy, the fabulous guy we met at Rothley who was an ex station master at the same time as Stuart Bailey (quoted in the ghost story book Railway Ghosts and Phantoms)

Strange figures have appeared at these arcaded entrance stairs, including that of a young boy who apparently fell down the stairs and died many years ago.

The ghost of an Edwardian lady has been seen in this waiting room.

This great little cafe overlooking the railway line also had a supernatural tale to tell. the middle part of the building (with the name written across) is very old and used to be a grain store. A short time ago a silver lid which sits unceremoniously on top of a coffee machine simply flew into the air and across the room!

Tamworth Castle, Staffordshire, and The Lady's Chamber

This room has seen more vigils than anywhere else in the castle. There are moving shadows, flickering lights, noises and cold spots. The "black lady" is said to haunt the room, possibly the spirit of Editha who also haunts the saircase.

This Haunted Staircase (which leads to the Tower Room), is where the ghost of Editha, King Alfred's granddaughter, is still said to appear. Apparently there have been various sounds of moans etc recorded on tape, and I myself actually made an audio recording of knocks I heard in response to my own. Although it is very quiet it is also tantalisingly audible, and if you're interested in hearing it for yourself please go to my facebook page or visit youtube.

Editha founded a convent here, but the nuns were eventually evicted by Robert de Marmion, who was given the castle by William the Conqueror. Editha was obviously not happy about this, and struck de Marmion with her crozier, causing a cut which continued to bleed until he swore to make amends.

The Ferrers Room

Staff often hear loud noises coming from this room, even when they know it is securely locked with no one inside. In 1999 the castle alarm went off, and the museum assistant while waiting for the engineer to arrive, could hear loud noises coming from this room which sounded like chairs and tables being dragged around. Frightened, she dashed outside to wait for the engineer. He was shocked to see her when he arrived as he had seen a figure standing in the Ferrers' Room window! When they investigated the room, nothing had been moved. Interestingly the room had been fitted that day with a new table and chairs, so perhaps the ghost wanted to rearrange the furniture a little!

The Drawing Room

The most well known ghostly sighting was by a museum assistant who sensed she was being watched and turned round to find a Victorian woman, dressed in black, sitting smiling at her on the green settee. The other ghosts that have been sighted in the room also appear to have been in Victorian dress.

Epworth Old Rectory - Birthplace of Methodism and Old Jeffrey the Poltergeist!

This beautiful rectory was the birthplace in 1703 of John Wesley, who along with his brother Charles founded the Methodist movement.

The house was rebuilt in 1709 after a fire destroyed the original property, and there was no reported ghostly activity until then. A tour guide at the property informed us that the family took in a homeless man called Jeffrey who helped in the gardens, and some time after he passed away here, the "disturbances" began.

It was a December night in 1716 that a servant heard a knock and what sounded like a groan. This happened three times, but on each occasion he went to the door, no-one was there. When he and the other servants went to bed, they found a handmill at the top of the stairs turning by itself. During the night there were other strange sounds. These "knocking" sounds (among others) continued, even Mrs Wesley who dismissed it all as nonsense at first, heard the sound of a cradle rocking in the nursery, even though there was no cradle there. The knocking also appeared to respond to the tapping of Samuel Wesley's walking stick.

The childen loved all the noises and chased the sounds from room to room. (While their large mastiff dog preferred to hide!)

A male ghost in a nightgown was seen, and also a creature Mrs Wesley described as a headless badger! Mr Wesley refused to leave the house, saying "he would not fly from the Devil".

By January 1717 the house was quiet again, and Old Jeffrey, or whatever had caused the disturbances, had apparently gone.

We felt that Epworth Rectory was a truly beautiful house that still has the feel of a family home.

Harlaxton Manor, near Grantham, Lincolnshire.

This beautiful building was started in 1832, and is currently a residential college owned by the University of Evansville, USA. It also has its fair share of ghosts...

The haunted library, where a previous owner Mrs Van der Elst held séances to contact her late husband. The room was later exorcised by Jesuits who had by then taken over the property.

RAF Coleby Grange, Metheringham, Lincolnshire.

This is just about all that remains of the night fighter station, which was in operation between 1941 and 1945. There have been reports of a ghostly airman and light anomalies. The commander of 409 squadron of the Royal Canadian Air Force was tragically killed after crash landing here.

I am quite interested in these particular light anomalies, as they can appear over marshes, swamps and boggy ground and are said to be caused by something called "bioluminescence". This is caused by the oxidation of chemicals produced by organic decay, and is witnessed as a ghostly light. It has also been known in folklore as "jack-o'-lantern" and "will-o'-the-wisp", and must be quite a strange sight if seen when wandering around in the dark. I have never witnessed them myself but believe them to be fairly common.

Temple Bruer, North Kesteven, Lincolnshire.

Associated with the Knights Templar, Henry VIII stayed here with his wife Katherine Howard on their way to Lincoln.

I make no apologies for the fact that Temple Bruer is not known to be haunted, as it is so uniquely beautiful and atmospheric. It is an extremely rare survival of standing remains of a Knight's Templar preceptory. The tower is believed to be one of a pair that once flanked the chancel at the east end of the preceptory church. The earliest parts of the church were built around 1160 with the surviving tower dating from about 1200.

What can I say about Temple Bruer? First that it was a devil to find as we must have driven right past it twice and had to ask for directions on more than one occasion, but then on discovering it for the first time.....what magic!

The interior on Temple Bruer - Blind arcading from the ground floor of the west wall. The last Grand Master of the English Templars, William de la More, was initiated here.

Unbelievably there appeared to be house building going on adjacent to the tower, and I could only think how lucky those people were to be living next door to a place such as this. It felt like something out of a sword and sorcery movie; mysterious and beautiful with jaw-dropping history. I climbed to the upper level just so that I could experience everything there was to see, and all I can say is that the tower is mesmerising.

We were observed on our visit by this enigmatic cat, who I would like to call "The Guardian of the Temple."

The Nell Gwyn, London.

This fab little pub is tucked down a narrow alley way called Bull Inn Court that leads off the Strand and is said to be haunted by the ghost of a past landlord.

A landlord during the 1990s went to a medium about the phenomena, (which included him being patted on the back trouser pocket!), and the medium told him that while the ghost was happy with how things were in the pub, then everything was fine - if the ghost wasn't happy then it would do its best to drive those reponsible away!

Several landlords of the Nell Gwyn have since tried to alter the pub's appearance, and all are said to have left for unknown reasons.

We asked the present bar staff if they had experienced anything "strange" recently - and they said they had!

Apparently just a few weeks ago several barrels fell over in the cellar for absolutely no reason, which obviously caused a bit of a fright. I heartily recommend this pub whether haunted or not, it was friendly, full of character and served a great dram of whisky!

The Ten Bells, near Spitalfields Market, London. (Jack the Ripper's Local Pub).

This beautiful old pub will forever be linked with the legend of Jack the Ripper who terrorised the city of London in the late 1800s. Its tiled wall panel shows how the area around the pub may have looked when there used to be countryside surrounding it.

Jack's final victim Mary Kelly left this pub on the 9th November 1888, and her body was discovered the following morning on the opposite side of the road.

The pub was renamed the Jack the Ripper during the 1970s and 1980s, but in 1989 it was returned to its original name, The Ten Bells. Live-in staff encountered the ghost of an old man in Victorian clothing who would lie next to them on the bed!

In June 2000 a new landlord cleared out the cellar and discovered an old metal box which held the personal effects of a man called George Roberts dating from the early 1900s. The items included a leather wallet which contained a press cutting that talked of his having been murdered with an axe in a Swansea cinema. Research showed that a man called George Roberts had kept the pub in the late 19th and early 20th centuries and the landlord reasoned that this man must be the ghost which haunted the building.

I walked Pete ragged trying to find this pub! It was a hot day as well so we were absolutely shattered by the time we found it, but it was worth it in the end.

Castle Rising – Norfolk.

Said to contain the ghost of Queen Isabella, who was prisoner here following her part in the murder of her husband Edward II, and the subsequent execution of her lover Mortimer.

Isabella's shrieks of maniacal laughter are still said to be heard within the castle. The only shrieking I heard was of kids running around, which was great for them but not so great for me.

I was actually trying to do a sound recording at the time, asking out "is anybody there?" The answer to that question was "yes, there is actually", but not specifically the type of "people" I was looking for. So after a good old search around this impressive castle we headed for the village café which was quintessentially idyllic, with a beautiful garden in which to imbibe copious amounts of coffee and of course a cream scone. Ah well, the exhausting demands of ghost hunting are never ending.....

St Marys Church at Woodford, Northamptonshire.

Inside a pillar in the north aisle behind a glass panel lies a carefully wrapped human heart. It is said to belong to the former vicar of the parish John Styles, who, due to his Catholic beliefs, was forced to flee. Around 1550 he fled to a monastery in Belgium, taking with him a valuable chalice from the church, and soon afterwards died there. A new vicar brought the chalice and John's heart back to Woodford several years later, but over the years both disappeared. In 1862 a ghost was seen in the hallway of the rectory, hovering near a panel in the wall. When examined, a secret hiding place was revealed, which contained the missing chalice and a letter, which detailed the whereabouts of John's heart within a pillar in the church. The heart can still be seen there to this day, wrapped in cloth. There is also said to be a ghostly figure which appeared to be kneeling at the altar, possibly the spirit of John Styles.

The Talbot Hotel, Oundle, Northamptonshire.

This reputedly haunted staircase is in the Talbot Hotel in Oundle, and was said to have been moved from Fotheringhay Castle where Mary Queen of Scots was beheaded. A portrait of Mary hangs just to the right of the staircase.

Featherstone Castle's Haunted Tower and Chapel near Alston, Northumberland

We were a little disappointed on arrival to find that Featherstone Castle is now a private residence and not open to the public, but we were incredibly fortunate that it is still open to paying guests, and these particular guests were quite happy to show us around the castle and its grounds, so many thanks for their warm hospitality.

They first of all told us about a ghost called Abigail who haunts the ruined chapel in the grounds, looking for her lost love. The chapel itself was a revelation and incredibly atmospheric, it was very easy to believe that a spirit frequented this area, but the biggest surprise was still to come.....

I had information on another ghost within the castle called Reginald FitzUrse, who had apparently been starved to death in the tower, and although he is perhaps not seen, his groans can still be heard. I relayed this story to the guests, of which they had never heard, and was stunned at their reaction.

One of the children within the group who was sleeping in a room beneath the tower, had asked one of the adults to check the tower just the previous night. She had been disturbed by what she said sounded like a man groaning in the room above her. They were not able to explore the room as it is locked. They knew absolutely nothing of the ghost within the tower story, and yet had experienced this just before our visit. I have tried on numerous occasions to contact the owner of the castle to try to gain access to do some investigations, but to no avail unfortunately. This has been one of the most intriguing personal accounts that I have ever discovered, so my hope remains that one day I will be able to return.

Llanbadrig, Anglesey, North Wales.

This is the site of Wylfa Nuclear Power Station. Whilst being built in 1964 workmen excavating a tunnel saw the apparition of a woman in white who hummed. This happened so frequently that several workmen resigned. It is the site of Galan Ddu, the Black Bank, the house in which Rosina Buckman, the New Zealand opera singer once lived. The casket containing her ashes is said to have been disturbed while the excavations were in progress.

Annesley Hall and Old Church, Nottinghamshire.

Annesley Hall is a Grade II listed country house near Annesley in Nottinghamshire which was the ancestral home of the Chaworth-Musters family. It dates from the 13th century. Mary Chaworth who lived at the hall was the childhood sweetheart of Lord Byron who lived close by at Newstead Abbey. It is now in a ruinous state and is unfortunately closed to the public. It has a huge reputation for being haunted.

Annesley Old Church overlooks the hall and is beautifully atmospheric. It is a grade I listed building and a scheduled ancient monument dating from the 12th century.

Old church, Annesley Hall.

The Bell Inn, Nottingham.

This ancient inn dates from around 1437 and claims to be the oldest pub in Nottingham (along with Ye Olde Trip to Jerusalem and The Salutation Inn). Carmelite Friars established a friary here in 1276 on what is now Friar Lane, which included a guest house on the site of what is now The Bell Inn. It became an ale house in 1539 following the Dissolution. The cellars are in both natural and hand carved caves in sandstone beneath the pub and date back to Norman times. They were excavated by the Carmelite Friars and contain two wells, from where the natural spring waters were once used for the brewing of beer. Perhaps some of the monks wished to remain; some staff have reported being touched by unseen hands and also having their names called when alone in the cellar!

The haunted bar area

Bestwood Lodge, Nottinghamshire.

Now a hotel, this fabulous gothic structure was once the residence of a royal hunting park, frequented by King Charles II and his mistress Nell Gwyn. It was demolished in 1860, and converted to a hotel in the mid 70's. Ghostly children have been heard crying and have also appeared at the hotel's glass front door, peering through into the hotel - but without a face... A small boy is sometimes seen in the bar area. The cellar and corridor is haunted by a man, and a lady has been seen in the hotel chapel, appearing to take her regular walk to prayer. Bestwood Lodge certainly appears to be one of the most haunted places in Nottinghamshire.

The Old Chapel.

Clifton Hall, Nottinghamshire.

I'm not sure if Clifton Hall exists of apartments or a single residence, but it's extremely private. It was owned in 2006 by Mr Rashid, a successful businessman. From the first night his family were aware of strange knocking sounds and a man's voice asking "is anyone there?" In the next 8 months that they remained at the house they continued to be haunted by the unexplained, and on the appearance of blood on their baby's quilt, they finally moved out. The owner of a security firm, Darren Brookes, said that while his company guarded the now empty house, some of his staff refused to work there. The hall has a 600 year history, including being a grammar school and an admin building for Nottingham Trent University, but has never before had a reputation for being haunted.

Colwick Hall, Nottingham.

During the 14th century Colwick Hall was the site of a manor house acquired by Lord Byron's ancestors. In 1643 the Byrons sold it to Sir John Musters. It was one of the Musters family that married Lady Mary Ann Chaworth, after her family rejected the marriage proposal of Lord Byron. He then found fame with his poetry and "dangerous" reputation. It is Lady Mary's ghost that is said to haunt the house and grounds, particularly along the grand mirrored corridor.

St Giles Church, Holme, Nottinghamshire – a visit to "Nan Scott's Chamber".

We last visited here in February last year but were unable to gain entry to the church. This time we managed to locate the key holder and discover a hidden gem - the actual room in which the legend of Ann Scott took shape. The porch window of the room in which she is believed to have incarcerated herself, is shown above the entrance to the church.

During the plague in the 17th century an elderly lady called Ann "Nan" Scott made it her dwelling place. When forced to visit her home for fresh supplies the parish was deserted save for one other person, and so she returned to the chamber to live out her days. Some say her footsteps can still be heard...

Nan Scott's Chamber in which she was said to have taken refuge from the Plague in the 17th century.

For a detailed account about her life, see - "Nan Scott - the face at the window" by Stan Smith. "A lone village widow who lived a hermits life in fear of the Great Plague". (Published by the John Merrill Foundation and part of the Nottinghamshire Heritage Series).

Nags Head, Mansfield Road, Nottingham.

This pub used to be an old coaching inn, where legend has it condemned prisoners were offered a last drink before being hanged nearby at Gallows Hill.

No such luck getting a drink here today as the landlord has apparently absconded!

Newstead Abbey, Nottinghamshire.

Ancestral home of Lord Byron and apparently home to a plethora of ghosts!

Byron was said to have actually witnessed the Black Friar (also known as the Goblin Friar), and also experienced several other paranormal events while sleeping in a bedchamber known as the Rook Cell. These included a black mass with glowing red eyes which sat on his bed - and a strange white mist which rose from the floor and then disappeared.

A White Lady ghost has been spotted in the gardens, and there is the scent of roses and lavender at the bottom of a certain staircase in the abbey.

I have attended a ghost hunt at the abbey which was incredibly interesting, and if you are into orbs there were more that showed up on my photos than you could shake a stick at. But if you're not into them, and I know people are seriously divided on this issue, then the "orbs", whatever they may be, will hold no interest.

I myself would like to reserve judgement on them for now. I agree that the vast majority of the time they are nothing more than light anomalies, my particular favourite being light reflected back onto the lens. But there have been others that looked decidedly different with bold outlines and patterns within them that showed themselves in what I considered to be paranormal "hot-spots". I took many photos in Newstead Abbey and one actually showed numerous orbs clustering around a spot on the wall where a sword had once hung that had been used by one of Byron's relatives. The sword had actually taken someone's life, so I thought this might be of particular importance.

We were also shown on another occasion Byron's bedroom by a member of staff who was also a lover of ghostly tales and the paranormal. She proceeded to continually "ask out" for whatever it was in the room to show itself, and we watched in amazement as strange marks or stains began appearing on the walls. It was like watching a mass of energy reshaping itself in front of us, and I have no idea how or why this was occurring, simply that it was.

The Crying Angel, East Stoke, Nottinghamshire.

In St Oswalds churchyard in East Stoke is the beautiful monument of an angel. It is the tomb of Baron Julian Pauncefoot, a local wealthy landowner, and the first ambassador that Britain sent to the USA. This angel has been seen to weep on even the driest of days, and no one knows how or why...

This forlorn looking yet beautiful statue put me in mind straight away of The Weeping Angels episode from Doctor Who, so I didn't like to look it in the eye for too long!

The Priory Church at Worksop in Nottinghamshire.

This beautiful church lays claim to having one of the oldest ghosts in Nottinghamshire, dating from the 1100s. The Black Canons established a priory here in 1103, dedicated to St Cuthbert, and the church is dominated by its two towers. It is on the top of one of these towers that the ghost of a monk appears, seemingly in great distress. He is seen to run around the tower and also peer over, as if watching and waiting...

There is also the ghost of a Blue Lady who is seen walking from the gatehouse to the church. Could there be a connection with the ghostly monk?

Rufford Abbey, Nottinghamshire and the Black Friar.

The site is said to be haunted by a monk, a hood hiding his ghostly face. The parish register for Edwinstowe even records the death of a man "from fright after seeing the Rufford ghost".A person who saw the reflection of the friar in a mirror described the clothing the ghost wore, and was told that it was not the habit of the monks who resided at the abbey many years ago, but was instead the habit of a monk who had once visited and subsequently died here.

There is also said to be a White Lady and a Victorian nanny pushing a pram who haunt the gardens. The White Lady is thought to be Lady Arabella Stuart, with Rufford Abbey being her childhood home. Arabella had been in distant line to the throne and so was considered a potential threat by King James who eventually had her imprisoned in the Tower of London, (after an unwise marriage that had been seen as confirmation of her dynastic ambitions). She escaped prison dressed as a boy but the ship on which she was escaping was captured near Dover and she was brought back to the Tower. When Arabella eventually died at 40 years of age, her ghost was said to have returned to Rufford Abbey, where hopefully she knew some happiness, and also I hope, managed to find some again.

Interior of the abbey, with a possible orb floating near the top of the photo!

The Bessie Sheppard Memorial Stone, Mansfield Road, Nottingham.

This stone marks the spot where 17 year old Elizabeth Sheppard was brutally murdered on the 7th July in 1817. Elizabeth was on her way to find work in Mansfield when she was attacked by Charles Rotherham, who thought she had money. He attacked her with a stake from the surrounding hedges. But all Elizabeth had of value were her shoes and umbrella, which Rotherham tried to sell at the Three Crowns Inn in Redhill. He was caught in Mansfield and later hanged on Gallows Hill in Nottingham. The Three Crowns Inn has since been demolished for new housing. Her ghost is said to haunt the spot whenever the stone is moved.

The Sunken Church, Bramcote, Nottinghamshire

The Domesday Book records a settlement here in "Bruncote" and a simple wooden structure is likely to have stood here before being rebuilt in stone.

The first known rector was in 1229.

It is known locally as the "Sunken Church" and was reputed to be haunted by a phantom monk. In 1978 the village policeman witnessed a strange figure in the churchyard. He observed it until it stopped by a gravestone, at which he then shone his torch towards it. But the beam of light shone through the shadow and straight onto the gravestone behind it. Then the figure began approaching the policeman in a gliding motion, but when the policeman drew closer the figure stopped and again retreated to a gravestone. The policeman had meanwhile radioed his inspector, who duly arrived, but by this time the figure had disappeared, and a search around the graveyard proved fruitless. The policeman described the figure as wearing a black ankle length coat and wearing some sort of three cornered hat with a high collar pulled underneath it. He could not see the face.

Shortly after his experience an elderly local gentleman came forward who believed that what had been seen was the ghost of a phantom coachman. He explained that many years ago a female servant in the village was killed by a coachman, who was so sorry for his crime that he committed suicide before he could be arrested, somewhere in the vicinity of the sunken church. His ghost is often mistaken for that of a monk, and was also witnessed by another two policemen on another night as they drove near the church.

The White Hart Pub in Lenton, Nottingham.

This pub was originally a farm in the 1600s, became coffee rooms in the early 1800s, and then a debtors' gaol. The site became a pub in 1897. There have been sightings of a ghostly man on the stairs, children singing and other unexplained shadows. The ghost is believed to be the jailor.

The windows of The White Hart Pub, which are still barred from its time as a debtors gaol in the 1800s. After enquiries in the pub we were told that due to redecorating work being carried out, spirit activity was again being experienced, particularly by the men carrying out the work. (Perhaps this is due to the Stone-tape theory? (I.e. memories being contained within the fabric of a building)

The Haunted "Holt Hotel", Steeple Aston, Oxfordshire.

We have just returned from a night in reputedly the most haunted room in the hotel - Room 3. Both this room and the hotel are said to be haunted by none other than the infamous Highwayman - Claude Du Vall, who was hung for his crimes at Tyburn in London aged 27 years in 1670.

Since 1475 The Holt Hotel (formerly Hopcroft Holt Inn) has been a resting place for weary travellers. Claude Du Vall used to frequent here, when it was a busy coaching inn. He was a French aristocrat born in 1643 who came to England and became a highwayman when times became hard. He was said to have an eye for the ladies, and allowed them to keep their jewels if they would dance with him (accompanied by his henchman on a mandolin!) .

He became so popular a figure that many noblewomen pleaded for his life - but Du Vall was found guilty of six robberies and was hung on the 21st Jan 1670 aged only 27 years old.

The bottle of wine in the photograph was obviously only there for dutch courage.

The stairway and corridor just outside the room are also said to be haunted, in which the sounds of heavy footsteps have been heard in the dead of night...i'm afraid I heard nothing as I wear earplugs. some noises in the night are more scary than even a ghosts heavy tread...

The Haunted Remains of Minster Lovell Hall, Witney, Oxfordshire.

Minster Lovell Hall and Dovecote were built by Lord William Lovell in the 1440's and dismantled in 1747.

Lord Lovell is said to be the ghost who haunts the hall, and he was a supporter of Lambert Simnel in 1487. (Lambert Simnel was a pretender to the English throne, who was trained to impersonate Richard, Duke of York, one of the princes murdered in the Tower of London.)

Lord Lovell rallied to the Yorkist cause, which culminated in the Battle of East Stoke in 1487. But the Yorkist's lost the battle to the Tudor King Henry VII.

Simnel was taken prisoner but pardoned and employed in the royal kitchen!

After the battle Lord Lovell went into hiding in a secret locked room, with only one servant taking care of him. But when this man died, Lord Lovell starved to death, and in 1718 when the house was being repaired, a vault was discovered in which a human skeleton was found seated at a table with a skeleton dog at its feet

The reluctant ghost hunter's trusty companion!

The Haunted Priory (which is now a private house.) Burford, Oxfordshire.

This impressive building used to be a priory for Anglo-Catholic nuns, while the chaplain lived in the Old Rectory nearby. Both houses were said to be "very haunted" with screams heard, singing near the monks' old graveyard, and a bell ringing at 2am. The ghosts of an old fashioned gamekeeper and a little brown monk have also been seen!

Unfortunately I was unable to get any closer to further investigate the property as it is now a private house with massive electric gates. So the ghosts (if they still remain) are well and truly hidden from public view.

Holy Trinity Church, Teigh, Rutland.

The village church at Teigh (pronounced "tea") in Rutland, where in 1321 Richard de Folville became the rector. He often joined his lawless and at that time out-lawed relations the Folvilles of Ashby Folville in Leicestershire and Newbold Folville in Huntingdon, in exploits of robbery and even murder. He eventually defended himself in Teigh church against the under-sheriff and his men, who overpowered him, dragged him out and cut off his head in the village street.

The Haunted Friary, East Bergholt, Suffolk.

The lovely village of East Bergholt contains what used to be a Benedictine convent. A door used to open by itself regularly at 10.50pm, along with a sharp drop of the temperature. A soldier who was staying here during the Second World War felt his face touched by cold hands, and overnight his hair turned white!

I would have loved to have entered the property to explore it further, but as is the case in so many of my "vintage" ghost books, the building is now privately owned and looked as if it had been turned into apartments. When I approached it closer to take a photograph a gentleman walked towards me from within the grounds and I asked him if it was still haunted. "Some say it is," was his enigmatic reply!

The "Green Children"

of Woolpit, Suffolk.

The sign for the village of Woolpit in Suffolk still portrays the local church, a wolf and two children painted green. The name of the village probably comes from "Wolf Pit" , when wolves still roamed the land many years ago, and when captured here were thrown into a pit. The green children though have an even stranger tale behind them. Sometime in the 12th century a boy and girl were said to have appeared from a hole in the ground, scared of the sun and their skin a strange colour of green. They couldn't speak English and so could not give any details of where they had come from. The boy soon died, but the girl lived and eventually married a local man. There have been many reasons given for the children's appearance - were they from an underground kingdom by the river? Were they fairies? Or perhaps it was simply due to a lack of iron, which can cause severe anaemia and give a green tinge to the skin. But the fairy tale story surrounding their miraculous appearance still exists to this day...

Rendlesham Forest UFO Trail, Suffolk.

One of the most celebrated UFO sightings ever in Britain took place here in December 1980 in Rendlesham Forest, a huge area of woodland between two RAF bases. On December 26th 1980 a local man reported seeing a glowing object in the sky, the same incident witnessed by two security men from RAF Woodbridge. They chased a small craft the size of a small car into the woods, where it hovered above the ground. It appeared to give off a "force-field" which prevented the two men approaching it, and actually caused their hair to stand on end. The following night Lt Col Charles Halt took a group of men from the base into the forest for further investigations. Shortly before 2am a "pyramid shaped object" which shone a bright white light appeared. The men chased this object through the forest for about an hour before it flew upwards and disappeared. The whole incident was recorded on audio tape. There is still controversy over what caused this amazing spectacle, as some people believe the lights were merely shining across from Orford Ness Lighthouse, emitting a brighter beam than they do today. But UFO hunters like myself still believe there is something more than heaven and earth out there...

Holy Trinity Church, Micklegate in York -

Which is said to be haunted by 3 ghosts - and also in York the grave of the notorious highwayman Dick Turpin!

I cannot recommend York highly enough, either to the seasoned ghost hunter or to anyone who loves history and atmosphere in equal measure. It's fabulous at any time of year and every time I go I seem to find somewhere I've not been before.

I had quite a rose-coloured image of Dick Turpin when I was a child, brought up as I was on tales of his daring exploits on Black Bess. He seemed almost legendary to me, like, dare I say it, Robin Hood, but just a bit darker. This idea I held of him was perpetuated by the 80s TV series of the same name, which simply added to his mystique. And then came a recent documentary in which my whole vision of Dick Turpin came crashing down to earth. The man was a nightmare! To say he was a bit of a devil would be an understatement, what a cruel let-down to my romantic imaginings.

Dick Turpin's Grave.

Holy Trinity Church, Micklegate, York.

Holy Trinity Church is lovely and well worth a visit, although I never saw or felt anything paranormal, and didn't like to ask. That is the awkward thing with supposedly haunted churches, I never wish to cause offence to anyone by asking if it's haunted! The church is also situated in a really pretty, tucked-away section of York, just opposite a fabulous bookshop, which is also perfect for whiling away your time in this amazing city.

Clapdale Hall (now a farmhouse), Clapham, North Yorkshire.

Many years ago there used to be a castle on this spot, owned by John de Clapham. It was haunted by the ghost of his foster mother, Dame Alice Kytell who became a witch.

I would have loved to question the owners of the farmhouse to discover if their building still retained any echoes from the past, but it appeared deserted apart from the resident flock of sheep!

Ardchattan Priory, Argyll.

Most of the buildings that survive here were built in the 15th and early 16th centuries when the existing church was enlarged. The Valliscaulian order of monks focused exclusively on the spiritual side of life, dedicated only to prayer and contemplation. They did no physical labour but lived off land rents, endowments and bequests.

No more than 20 monks were allowed in a community, and here at Ardchattan there were periods when only 3 monks were living here.

A nun from Kilmaronaig Convent was said to be smuggled into Ardchattan Priory and hidden under the floor of the oratory, where her remains still lie. Why this poor nun would have been smuggled here in the first place tradition does not state, but it certainly provides more than enough grounds for a haunting...

Ardvreck Castle, Loch Assynt.

Encircled by the Quinag peaks, the Inchnadamph forest and a nature reserve, Ardvreck Castle is in an absolutely stunning location. Nearby are the famous Inchnadamph Bone Caves, where the bones of reindeer, bears, arctic foxes, lynx and even polar bears were discovered, dating from around 45,000 years ago.

The castle was built around the late 1500s, and in 1650 the Royalist James Graham, the Marquess of Montrose, was somehow talked into entering its dungeon on a false pretext, and then sent to be executed in Edinburgh. This castle is still said to harbour his ghost, and I'm not surprised. I only hope if his ghost is here that it doesn't still languish in the dungeon but is admiring the heart-stopping views, which embrace you here as if you're in some sort of romantic dream. Every scene is inspiration for yet another shortbread biscuit tin...

Ballachulish House, Glencoe.

Said to be the most haunted house in Scotland, and where the wake for James Stewart was held, it has been the seat of the Stewarts of Ballachulish since the 16th century, and was also where the final order for the Glencoe Massacre was signed.

It is now a hotel/guest house, with a lot of stories to tell I'm sure. The building looked empty and in darkness when we arrived to take a look, so I satisfied myself with just a picture and the intention to return very soon and actually stop overnight. Glencoe and the surrounding area is our favourite part of Scotland and we usually holiday here at least once a year. It would be hard to find somewhere more majestically beautiful than these stunning mountains.

Barcaldine Castle; Haunted by its 18th century laird - and a Blue Lady!

The beautiful and picturesque Barcaldine Castle is said to be haunted by the ghost of Donald Campbell, who for years had been involved in a feud with Stewart of Appin. The dispute came to a terrible end when Stewart killed Donald with his sword, upon which Stewart amazingly sought refuge with Donald's brother at Inverawe. (Donald's brother Duncan had not yet heard of the murder and so offered Stewart his hospitality.)

Duncan was haunted by visions of his brother, but by the time he discovered Donald was dead and that the visions were actually his ghost, Stewart had gone. Duncan's ghost still haunts Inverawe, but Donald's ghost returned to Barcaldine, an angry spirit that returns from time to time, still wanting his revenge on Stewart of Appin.

Barcaldine Castle is also said to be haunted by a Blue Lady who loves music. I would have loved to have had a look round the castle, but there were signs outside stating that it was a private residence and actually now run as a luxury bed and breakfast! Perhaps another time.....

Corgaff Castle, Aberdeenshire.

It is hard to imagine that so much tragedy happened here in such beautiful surroundings, but in November 1571 Adam Gordon of Auchindoun (who supported the deposed Mary, Queen of Scots), came with his men to take the castle for the Queen.

The Forbes family who lived here supported Mary's son James VI, and Margaret Forbes, the wife of the laird, refused them entry. So they set the castle alight, and Margaret and her family and servants were burnt to death. In all about 24 people died. Now I know some places are known for ghosts and some aren't, and I must admit that as far as I'm aware Corgaff Castle isn't haunted. But if ghosts do exist I find it hard to imagine that they wouldn't be haunting here. The castle is certainly in a very stark, barren location, and although the scenery looked quite beautiful in the setting sun, I was struck by just how truly isolated it is.

It felt like quite an unforgiving atmosphere, and seemed more like the barracks it became rather than the home it once was, however grand. Places like Corgaff Castle raise my passionate interest in the Stone-tape theory, in which the memories of certain dramatic events may seep into the walls and very fabric of the building. Therefore when the walls are "broken" in any way (such as during renovation work) these memories can be released and seen as a physical presence by whoever happens to be there at the time, a particular case in point being the Roman army seen walking through a wall in York when major work was being carried out in the cellars. At some point I would love to write a book regarding work-men and women's experiences of the paranormal while carrying out their jobs, because if the Stone-tape theory is to be believed, they would be the ideal candidates to discover more about it. Builders in particular must be a valuable un-tapped source of information as far as I'm concerned, so please get in touch if this applies to you!

The Drover's Inn, Inverarnan, Loch Lomond.
(Est. 1705)

Is this the most haunted hotel in Britain? I have never stopped here overnight so I'm unable to answer for myself. And what do you mean why haven't I stopped here, the title of the book is the "reluctant" ghost hunter remember. I am slowly picking up courage to stretch myself a little more in my search for answers to the paranormal, but not quite ready for this one yet. The Drover's Inn is an amazingly cosy, atmospheric place, but also very dark and a little bit forbidding. My memory of the stuffed animals that once filled the reception area also stays in my mind.

There are tales of lights going on and off, the spirit of a child, and a ghostly cattle drover who was murdered.

This pub/hotel has got to be one of the "must-see" places to visit in Scotland, complete with real open fires and a feeling that you have stepped back in time, (or on somebody's grave).....

Orbs.

If there is one subject that is guaranteed to get members of the paranormal community hot under the collar, it's orbs. There has been reams written about them and countless websites devoted to them. They have been described as having various meanings, chiefly among the many interpretations is that of angels and loved ones in spirit looking after us from beyond. I myself have got extremely excited about them, particularly when I have attended a ghost walk and the orb shape looks particularly "solid". I was struck though as to why the orbs seemed to stop appearing as soon as I purchased a new camera. Suddenly there were no more orbs, the only exceptions being when light was reflected on the lens or evening shots of rain or snow (see photo below taken at Robin Hood's Bay as an example). I wonder if orbs only show up on "vintage" cameras rather than modern digital ones. Some investigators believe that analogue eqpt such as tape recorders may record paranormal evidence in a way far superior to brand new expensive technology, so could this relate to cameras also? Again, I would be very interested if any readers would get in touch if they have any good examples regarding this. I think there should be a lot more discussion regarding some of these subjects, and people should not be afraid of coming forward with their own evidence or ideas. This is the only way I believe we will be able to move forward in our investigations of the paranormal world with any degree of clarity.

Footnote

Many thanks to everyone who has taken the time to pick up this book and take a dive into my personal take on the paranormal world that surrounds us. I love the fact that we don't have the answers to everything, and wouldn't life be boring if we did? But I am also sure that we are meant to question the strange things that happen to us sometimes, or else why would they happen in the first place?

I have had to seriously reduce the amount of photographs and detail that I would have loved to have included, but if you would like to peruse my Facebook page "the reluctant ghost hunter" you will find a lot more information there, including more on my interest in our fabulous history and folklore.

We are so lucky living on this fabulous isle to have such a wealth of treasures around us, whether it be beautiful villages, majestic mountains or simply our amazing and varied history. I never want my search to stop for new and mysterious places, and while I am able to do so I will continue to explore this amazing country of Great Britain, one I am so pleased and proud to call home.

With Thanks.

There are so many people I would like to thank for their help, support and inspiration. If I miss anyone out I apologise profusely, but you know who you are.

Tom Warrington, what a star, you have supported my endeavours right from the start, including asking me several times onto the Pure Paranormal Radio Show which Tom co-hosts with Barry Frankish on Pulse Talk Radio.

Christine, my fab friend, you have not only given me numerous paranormal books but also been generous enough to tell me your own experiences of the paranormal. You even supported me on my one and only organised ghost hunt (so far!) at the Guildhall in Leicester.

Linda, love and light to you my friend – thank you so much for your unwavering friendship and support.

Joyce, with your belief in me I felt that I could do anything, thank you and much love.

The author Stuart Laing, who I am also lucky enough to call a friend. You have given me so much support and encouragement through Facebook etc., I can't thank you enough.

Richard, thank you so much for giving me the brilliant book "Haunted Britain", which has inspired the majority of my travels.

Marion and Dee from Leicester Progressive Spiritualist Church, love and thanks for your fabulous help and support on the evening of my "Spirited Soiree" at the Leicester Guildhall.

All my Facebook friends who like and support my posts, I am honoured to call you "friends".

The author Rupert Matthews who took the time and trouble to respond to my email and give me valuable pointers on putting this book together in the first place.

And finally, and most importantly, I want to thank my husband Pete. You have made every step of my journey so far more exciting, more light-hearted, and more joyful than I could ever have imagined. Much as much xxx

Bibliography

If I have omitted anyone, my sincerest apologies, please get in touch so that your name can be added on the next edition.

Coxe Hippisley - A. Haunted Britain.

W.B. Herbert - Railway Ghosts and Phantoms

Rosemary Robb - Ghost Hunting & Ghosts and Legends of Newark ..

Joanne Brown and John Dickinson - The Ghosts of Grace Dieu.

Tamworth Borough Council - The Ghosts of Tamworth Castle.

Rupert Matthews - The Ghosthunter's Guide to England.

Betty Puttick - Supernatural England.

Richard Jones - Haunted London.

Len Moakes - Haunted Nottinghamshire Vol 2.

David Brandon - Haunted Bath, Haunted Chester & Haunted Lincoln.

Andrew James Wright - Haunted Leicester & Haunted Nottingham.

Jill Armitage - Haunted Places of Derbyshire & Derbyshire Ghost Stories & Haunted Places of Nottinghamshire.

Richard Holland - Oxfordshire Ghost Stories.

Stuart Andrews and Jaso Higgs - Paranormal Cornwall .

Margaret Caine and Alan Gorton - Cornwall's Haunted Houses

Lily Seafield - Scottish Ghosts.

E. Frank Earp. - The A-Z of Curious Nottinghamshire.

Wikipedia (Information on light anomalies.)

The Ghost and Legend Series.

DERBYSHIRE & THE PEAK DISTRICT -
Legends of Derbyshire by Revd. John N. Merrill
Derbyshire Folklore by Revd. John N. Merrill
Customs of Derbyshire & The Peak District by Revd. John N. Merrill
Punishment in Derbyshire by Revd. John N. Merrill

ESSEX -
Essex Witch Walks - Revd. John N. Merrill

NOTTINGHAMSHIRE -
Ghost Hunting around Nottinghamshire by Rosemary Robb
Ghosts and Legends of Newark by Rosemary Robb
The Restless Spirit - more Ghost & Legends by Rosemary Robb
Wartime Ghost Stories and Mysteries by Rosemary Robb
A Ghostly Guide to Nottinghamshire by Catherine Staton
Rhyme & Reason - some Nottinghamshire Folk tales by Ztan Zmith
Bell Tales - by Ztan Zmith

LINCOLNSHIRE -
Ghost Stories from North Lincolnshire by Stephen Wade.
Lincolnshire Hauntings by Sean Mcneaney.

YORKSHIRE -
True Ghost Stories from Leeds by Chris Wade.

GREAT BRITAIN -
Travels with a Reluctant Ghost Hunter by Joanna Jackson Cowell

FOR A FULL DETAILS OF OUR PUBLICATIONS VISIT -
WWW.JOHNMERRILLWALKGUIDES.CO.UK
WWW.PILGRIMSBOOKSHOP.COM

THE JOHN MERRILL FOUNDATION
WALTHAM CROSS, HERTFORDSHIRE. EN8 8QY
EMAIL - MARATHONHIKER@AOL.COM

The Nottinghamshire Heritage Series -

BELL TALES by Ztan Zmith

SOME NOTTINGHAMSHIRE PUB STORIES by Ztan Zmith

RHYME AND REASON - some Nottinghamshire Folk Tales by Ztan Zmith

WHAT A LIFE by Ztan Zmith

NAN SCOTT - the face at the window by Ztan Zmith

HISTORY OF SUTTON IN ASHFIELD - facsimile of 1907 edition

LORD BYRON" Mad, bad and dangerous to know."- by E. Eisenberg

THE OLD NORTH ROAD by Joan Board

ATO Z OF PILGRIM COUNTRY by Joan Board

THE GREAT NOTH ROAD THROUGH NOTTINGHAMSHIRE ny Joan Board

WOLLATON HALL by Elizabeth May - Wollaton was a family home and Natural History Museum

BASFORD - Village to Suburb by A.S.Bowley

RAILWAYS REMEMBERED - Basford & Bulwell - 1848 - 1967 by Ashley R. Durose.

LOOKING UP AT NOTTINGHAM Walks nos. |,2,3,4,5,6,7,8,& 9 - historical city walks - 1 to 2 miles long by Terence White

THE VILLAGE OF ELKESLEY - a comprehensive history by Alan Hirst.

THE JOHN MERRILL FOUNDATION,
32, Holmesdale,
Waltham Cross, Herts. EN8 8QY
www.johnmerrillwalkguides.co.uk

OTHER BOOKS by Revd. John N. Merrill

CIRCULAR WALK GUIDES -

SHORT CIRCULAR WALKS IN THE PEAK DISTRICT - Vols. 1 to 9
CIRCULAR WALKS IN WESTERN PEAKLAND
SHORT CIRCULAR WALKS IN THE STAFFORDSHIRE MOORLANDS
SHORT CIRCULAR WALKS - TOWNS & VILLAGES OF THE PEAK DISTRICT
SHORT CIRCULAR WALKS AROUND MATLOCK
SHORT CIRCULAR WALKS IN "PEAK PRACTICE COUNTRY."
SHORT CIRCULAR WALKS IN THE DUKERIES
SHORT CIRCULAR WALKS IN SOUTH YORKSHIRE
SHORT CIRCULAR WALKS IN SOUTH DERBYSHIRE
SHORT CIRCULAR WALKS AROUND BUXTON
SHORT CIRCULAR WALKS AROUND WIRKSWORTH
SHORT CIRCULAR WALKS IN THE HOPE VALLEY
40 SHORT CIRCULAR WALKS IN THE PEAK DISTRICT
CIRCULAR WALKS ON KINDER & BLEAKLOW
SHORT CIRCULAR WALKS IN SOUTH NOTTINGHAMSHIRE
SHORT CIRCULAR WALKS IN CHESHIRE
SHORT CIRCULAR WALKS IN WEST YORKSHIRE
WHITE PEAK DISTRICT AIRCRAFT WRECKS
CIRCULAR WALKS IN THE DERBYSHIRE DALES
SHORT CIRCULAR WALKS FROM BAKEWELL
SHORT CIRCULAR WALKS IN LATHKILL DALE
CIRCULAR WALKS IN THE WHITE PEAK
SHORT CIRCULAR WALKS IN EAST DEVON
SHORT CIRCULAR WALKS AROUND HARROGATE
SHORT CIRCULAR WALKS IN CHARNWOOD FOREST
SHORT CIRCULAR WALKS AROUND CHESTERFIELD
SHORT CIRCULAR WALKS IN THE YORKS DALES - Vol 1 - Southern area.
SHORT CIRCULAR WALKS IN THE AMBER VALLEY (Derbyshire)
SHORT CIRCULAR WALKS IN THE LAKE DISTRICT
SHORT CIRCULAR WALKS IN THE NORTH YORKSHIRE MOORS
SHORT CIRCULAR WALKS IN EAST STAFFORDSHIRE
LONG CIRCULAR WALKS IN THE PEAK DISTRICT - Vol.1 to 5.
DARK PEAK AIRCRAFT WRECK WALKS
LONG CIRCULAR WALKS IN THE STAFFORDSHIRE MOORLANDS
LONG CIRCULAR WALKS IN CHESHIRE
WALKING THE TISSINGTON TRAIL
WALKING THE HIGH PEAK TRAIL
WALKING THE MONSAL TRAIL & SETT VALLEY TRAILS
PEAK DISTRICT WALKING - TEN "TEN MILER'S" - Vol 1 and 2.
CLIMB THE PEAKS OF THE PEAK DISTRICT
PEAK DISTRICT WALK A MONTH Vols One,Two, Three, Four, Five & Six
TRAIN TO WALK Vol. One - The Hope Valley Line
DERBYSHIRE LOST VILLAGE WALKS -Vol One and Two.
CIRCULAR WALKS IN DOVEDALE AND THE MANIFOLD VALLEY
CIRCULAR WALKS AROUND GLOSSOP
WALKING THE LONGDENDALE TRAIL
WALKING THE UPPER DON TRAIL
SHORT CIRCULAR WALKS IN CANNOCK CHASE
CIRCULAR WALKS IN THE DERWENT VALLEY
WALKING THE TRAILS OF NORTH-EAST DERBYSHIRE
WALKING THE PENNINE BRIDLEWAY & CIRCULAR WALKS
SHORT CIRCULAR WALKS ON THE NEW RIVER & SOUTH-EAST HERTFORDSHIRE
SHORT CIRCULAR WALKS IN EPPING FOREST
SHORT CIRCULAR WALKS AROUND SAFFRON WALDEN
LONG CIRCULAR WALKS AROUND HERTFORD

WALKING THE STREETS OF LONDON
LONG CIRCULAR WALKS IN EASTERN HERTFORDSHIRE
LONG CIRCULAR WALKS IN WESTERN HERTFORDSHIRE
WALKS IN THE LONDON BOROUGH OF ENFIELD
WALKS IN THE LONDON BOROUGH OF BARNET
WALKS IN THE LONDON BOROUGH OF HARINGEY
WALK IN THE LONDON BOROUGH OF WALTHAM FOREST
SHORT CIRCULAR WALKS AROUND HERTFORD
THE BIG WALKS OF LONDON
SHORT CIRCULAR WALKS AROUND BISHOP'S STORTFORD
SHORT CIRCULAR WALKS AROUND EPPING DISTRICT
CIRCULAR WALKS IN THE BOROUGH OF BROXBOURNE
LONDON INTERFAITH WALKS - Vol 1 and Vol. 2
LONG CIRCULAR WALKS IN THE NORTH CHILTERNS
SHORT CIRCULAR WALKS IN EASTERN HERTFORDSHIRE
WORCESTERSHIRE VILLAGE WALKS by Des Wright
WARWICKSHIRE VILLAGE WALKS by Des Wright
WALKING AROUND THE ROYAL PARKS OF LONDON
WALKS IN THE LONDON BOROUGH OF CHELSEA AND ROYAL KENSINGTON
ESSEX WITCH WALKS.

CANAL WALKS -

VOL 1 - DERBYSHIRE & NOTTINGHAMSHIRE
VOL 2 - CHESHIRE & STAFFORDSHIRE
VOL 3 - STAFFORDSHIRE
VOL 4 - THE CHESHIRE RING
VOL 5 - THE GRANTHAM CANAL
VOL 6 - SOUTH YORKSHIRE
VOL 7 - THE TRENT & MERSEY CANAL
VOL 8 - WALKING THE DERBY CANAL RING
VOL 9 - WALKING THE LLANGOLLEN CANAL
VOL 10 - CIRCULAR WALKS ON THE CHESTERFIELD CANAL
VOL 11 - CIRCULAR WALKS ON THE CROMFORD CANAL
Vol.13 - SHORT CIRCULAR WALKS ON THE RIVER LEE NAVIGATION -Vol. 1 - North
Vol. 14 - SHORT CIRCULAR WALKS ON THE RIVER STORT NAVIGATION
Vol.15 - SHORT CIRCULAR WALKS ON THE RIVER LEE NAVIGATION - Vol. 2 - South
Vol. 16 - WALKING THE CANALS OF LONDON
Vol 17 - WALKING THE RIVER LEE NAVIGATION
Vol. 20 - SHORT CIRCULAR WALKS IN THE COLNE VALLEY
Vol 21 - THE BLACKWATER & CHELMER NAVIGATION - End to End.
Vol. 22 - NOTTINGHAM'S LOST CANAL by Bernard Chell.
Vol. 23 - WALKING THE RIVER WEY & GODALMING NAVIAGTIONS END TO END
Vol.25 - WALKING THE GRAND UNION CANAL - LONDON TO BIRMINGHAM.

JOHN MERRILL DAY CHALLENGE WALKS

WHITE PEAK CHALLENGE WALK
THE HAPPY HIKER - WHITE PEAK - CHALLENGE WALK
DARK PEAK CHALLENGE WALK
PEAK DISTRICT END TO END WALKS
STAFFORDSHIRE MOORLANDS CHALLENGE WALK

JOHN MERRILL DAY CHALLENGE WALKS

WHITE PEAK CHALLENGE WALK No. 1
THE HAPPY HIKER - WHITE PEAK CHALLENGE WALK No.2
DARK PEAK CHALLENGE WALK
PEAK DISTRICT END TO END WALKS
STAFFORDSHIRE MOORLANDS CHALLENGE WALK
THE LITTLE JOHN CHALLENGE WALK
YORKSHIRE DALES CHALLENGE WALK
NORTH YORKSHIRE MOORS CHALLENGE WALK
LAKELAND CHALLENGE WALK
THE RUTLAND WATER CHALLENGE WALK
MALVERN HILLS CHALLENGE WALK
THE SALTERiS WAY
THE SNOWDON CHALLENGE
CHARNWOOD FOREST CHALLENGE WALK
THREE COUNTIES CHALLENGE WALK (Peak District).
CAL-DER-WENT WALK
THE QUANTOCK WAY
BELVOIR WITCHES CHALLENGE WALK
THE CARNEDDAU CHALLENGE WALK
THE SWEET PEA CHALLENGE WALK
THE LINCOLNSHIRE WOLDS - BLACK DEATH - CHALLENGE WALK
JENNIFER'S CHALLENGE WALK
THE EPPING FOREST CHALLENGE WALK
THE THREE BOROUGH CHALLENGE WALK - N.LONDON
THE HERTFORD CHALLENGE WALK
THE BOSHAM CHALLENGE WALK
THE KING JOHN CHALLENGE WALK
THE NORFOLK BROADS CHALLENGE WALK
THE RIVER MIMRAM WALK
THE ISLE OF THANET CHHALENGE WALK
EAST DEVON CHALLENGE WALK
THE SANDSTONE ROCKS CHALLENGE WALK
MATTERHON CHALLENGE WALK
PORTLAND BILL CHALLENGE WALK
ESSEX WITCH'S CAHLLENGE WALK

INSTRUCTION & RECORD -

HIKE TO BE FIT.....STROLLING WITH JOHN
THE JOHN MERRILL WALK RECORD BOOK
HIKE THE WORLD - John Merrill's guide to walking & Backpacking.

MULTIPLE DAY WALKS -

THE RIVERS'S WAY
PEAK DISTRICT: HIGH LEVEL ROUTE
PEAK DISTRICT MARATHONS
THE LIMEY WAY
THE PEAKLAND WAY
COMPO'S WAY by Alan Hiley
THE BRIGHTON WAY

COAST WALKS & NATIONAL TRAILS -

ISLE OF WIGHT COAST PATH
PEMBROKESHIRE COAST PATH
THE CLEVELAND WAY
WALKING ANGELSEY'S COASTLINE.
WALKING THE COASTLINE OF THE CHANNEL ISLANDS
THE ISLE OF MAN COASTAL PATH - "The Way of the Gull."
A WALK AROUND HAYLING ISLAND
A WALK AROUND THE ISLE OF SHEPPEY
A WALK AROUND THE ISLE OF JERSEY
WALKING AROUND THE ISLANDS OF ESSEX
WALKING AROUND ESSEX'S COASTLINE - 320 MILES

DERBYSHIRE & PEAK DISTRICT HISTORICAL GUIDES -

A to Z GUIDE OF THE PEAK DISTRICT
DERBYSHIRE INNS - an A to Z guide
HALLS AND CASTLES OF THE PEAK DISTRICT & DERBYSHIRE
TOURING THE PEAK DISTRICT & DERBYSHIRE BY CAR
DERBYSHIRE FOLKLORE
PUNISHMENT IN DERBYSHIRE
CUSTOMS OF THE PEAK DISTRICT & DERBYSHIRE
WINSTER - a souvenir guide
ARKWRIGHT OF CROMFORD
LEGENDS OF DERBYSHIRE
DERBYSHIRE FACTS & RECORDS
TALES FROM THE MINES by Geoffrey Carr
PEAK DISTRICT PLACE NAMES by Martin Spray
DERBYSHIRE THROUGH THE AGES - Vol 1 -DERBYSHIRE IN PREHISTORIC TIMES
SIR JOSEPH PAXTON
FLORENCE NIGHTINGALE
JOHN SMEDLEY
BONNIE PRINCE CHARLIE & 20 mile walk.
THE STORY OF THE EARLS AND DUKES OF DEVONSHIRE

JOHN MERRILL'S MAJOR WALKS -

TURN RIGHT AT LAND'S END
WITH MUSTARD ON MY BACK
TURN RIGHT AT DEATH VALLEY
EMERALD COAST WALK
I CHOSE TO WALK - Why I walk etc.
A WALK IN OHIO - 1,310 miles around the Buckeye Trail.
I AM GUIDED - the story of John's wallking life.

SKETCH BOOKS -

SKETCHES OF THE PEAK DISTRICT

COLOUR BOOK:-

THE PEAK DISTRICT.......something to remember her by.

OVERSEAS GUIDES -

HIKING IN NEW MEXICO - Vol I - The Sandia and Manzano Mountains.
Vol 2 - Hiking "Billy the Kid" Country.
Vol 4 - N.W. area - " Hiking Indian Country."
"WALKING IN DRACULA COUNTRY" - Romania.
WALKING THE TRAILS OF THE HONG KONG ISLANDS.

VISITOR GUIDES - MATLOCK . BAKEWELL.

ASHBOURNE.

CYCLING - PARIS TO MT. ST. MICHEL & ST. MALO.

WALTHAM ABBEY TO BARKING ABBEY